AMERICA:

Beautifully Unique

Devon Goddard
Lindsay Robertson

For the families who helped to pave the way before us and for the children we have lost too soon along the way.

50 STATES

Washington

Oregon

Idaho

Montana

North Dakota

South Dakota

Wyoming

Nebraska

Nevada

Utah

Colorado

Kansas

California

Arizona

New Mexico

Oklahoma

Texas

Alaska

OF AMERICA

nnesota

Wisconsin

Michigan

wa

Illinois

Indiana

souri

Kentucky

Tennessee

ansas

Alabama

Louisiana

Mississippi

Vermont

Maine

New Hampshire

New York

Massachusetts

Rhode Island

Pennsylvania

New Jersey

Delaware

Connecticut

Virginia

Ohio

North Carolina

South Carolina

Georgia

Maryland

West Virginia

Florida

Washington D.C.

Hawaii

POPCORN INDIANA

LONG LIVE ROCK

ALABAMA

Montgomery

The "Heart of Dixie" is
where the tribes used to roam,
but for cotton, chickens, cattle and calves,
it's home sweet home!

(Model : Seth, Jacksonville)

ALASKA

Juneau

Alaska is the largest state,
surrounded by water on most sides.
Forests filled with spruce trees,
where moose and bears hide!

(Model : Sarah, Eagle River)

ARIZONA

Phoenix

Arizona is home to the Grand Canyon,
many miles deep and wide.
The sun beats hot, the deserts dry,
and the cacti thrive!

(Model : Ryder, Scottsdale)

ARKANSAS

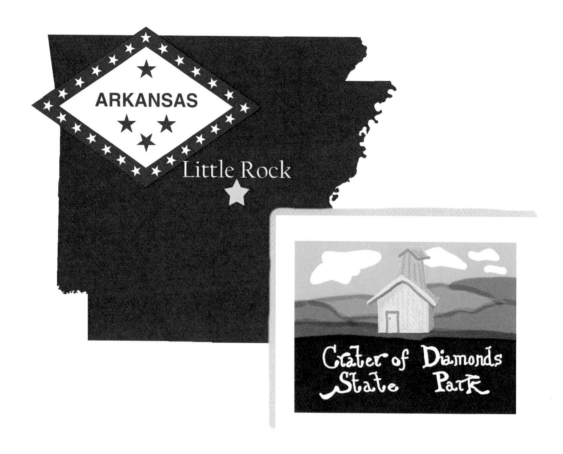

Crater of Diamonds State Park

Natural beauty is what you'll find here,
in the state of the white-tailed deer.
Our country counts on Arkansas,
for natural resources that help us all!

(Model : Gretchen, Van Buren)

CALIFORNIA

Venture through the Redwood Forest,
surf down the sunny coast,
sail under the Golden Gate Bridge,
this state is visited most.
Pistachios, almonds, lemons, and peaches,
the farmers are busy while tourists
enjoy the beaches!

(Model : Beckett, San Diego)

COLORADO

With deep valleys and mountain peaks,
this is the place to be.
Colorado is an adventurous place-
grab your hiking boots and skis!

(Models : Lila and Lexi, Littleton)

CONNECTICUT

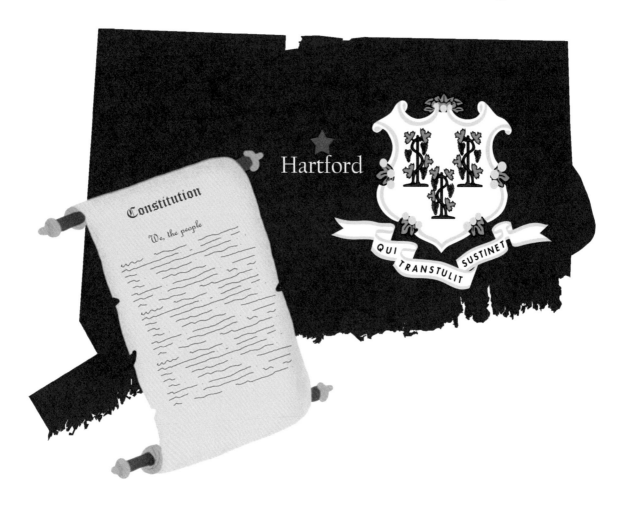

The constitution state is full of history,
like the USS Nautilus and Mark Twain.
Split in half by a river,
with hills and deep forests,
the nature here is insane!

(Model : Sam, Mystic)

DELAWARE

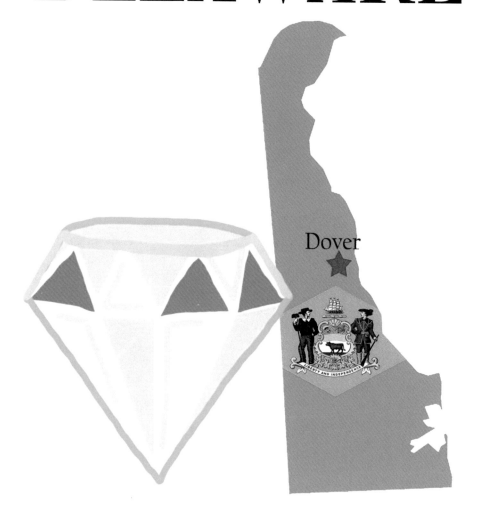

Dover

Blue hen chickens, NASCAR races,
and the southern sandy beaches.
Being the very first state,
there's so much history that Delaware teaches!

(Model : Clara, Camden)

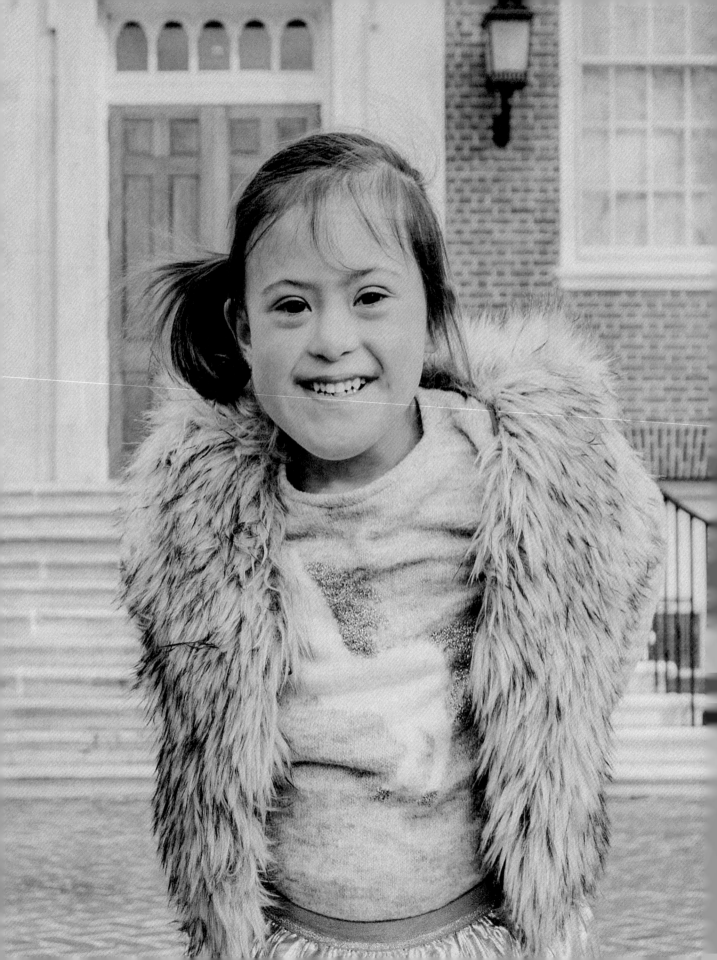

FLORIDA

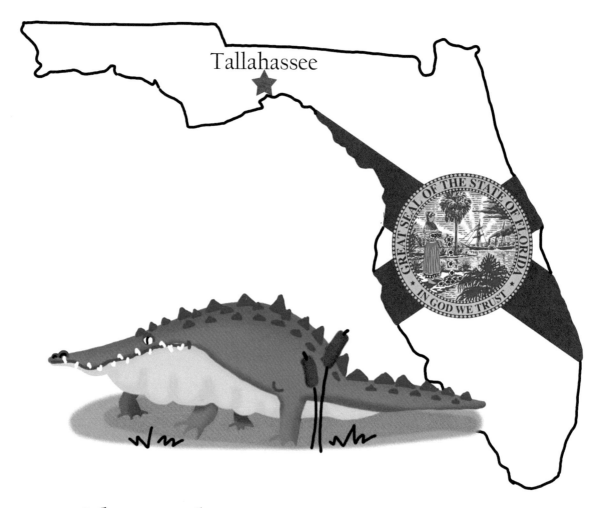

Tallahassee

The Sunshine State is exactly that;
full of sun, sand, and flowers.
Travel from St. Augustine to the Everglades;
but don't forget to watch for gators,
their teeth are sharp as blades!

(Model : Charlotte, Jacksonville)

GEORGIA

Atlanta

Georgia is home to the largest swamp,
but it's known for much sweeter treats.
Vidalia onions, peanuts, and peaches;
everyone comes and eats!

(Model: Paisley, Valdosta)

HAWAII

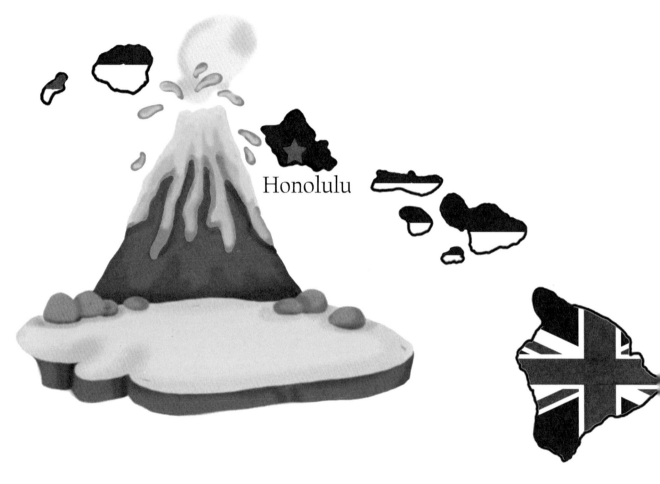

Honolulu

The Aloha state grew out of the ocean,
the active volcanoes caused quite the commotion.
Monk seals, fish, and exotic flowers,
it's a tropical paradise that
can be explored for hours!

(Model : Kahiau, Ewa Beach)

IDAHO

Although Idaho is known for its potatoes,
fishing is what it's all about.
Float across the state on the Snake River
and catch yourself some trout!

(Model : Ronin, Coeur d'Alene)

ILLINOIS

Springfield

Chicago, the windy city,
is home to the Willis Tower.
Being the tallest building in North America,
climbing it could take over an hour.
Outside of the city, you will see,
miles of corn growing wild and free!

(Model : Cameron, Loves Park)

INDIANA

Indianapolis

WELCOME TO
POPCORN
INDIANA
POPULATION 42

Indiana is known as the Hoosier State,
and has beautiful tulip trees.
The Indy 500 is their big event-
these drivers make it look like a breeze!

(Model: Eleanor, Mitchell)

IOWA

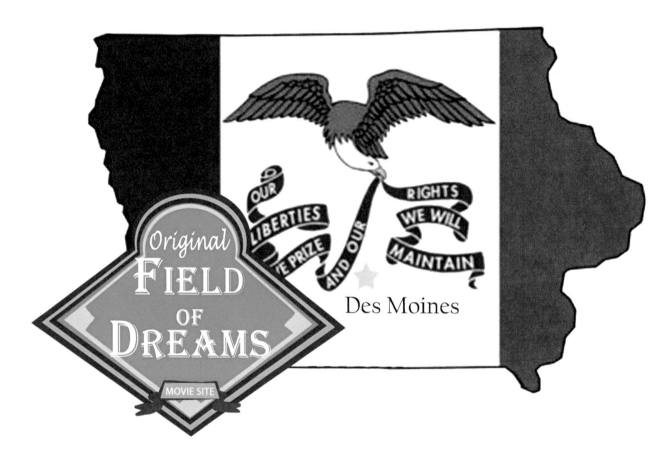

Des Moines

The Iowa Caucus is the start
of every presidential race,
but there's a lot more to this wonderful place.
Known for its fertile soil, oats, and hay-
the land in Iowa makes farmers want to stay!

(Model: CJ, Sioux City)

KANSAS

Topeka

This state used to be a sea,
but with the Red and Smokey Hills there
now it cannot be.
The land is very flat,
with tall sunflowers and wheat-
and the natural beauty here can't be beat!

(Model : Anistyn, Hoxie)

KENTUCKY

Frankfort

COMMONWEALTH OF KENTUCKY

UNITED WE STAND

DIVIDED WE FALL

Home to Red River Gorge and Mammoth Cave,
Kentucky's bluegrass is all the rave.
Cardinals flutter and fly about,
and the Kentucky Derby is where tourists go,
day in and day out!

(Model: Levi, Mount Sterling)

LOUISIANA

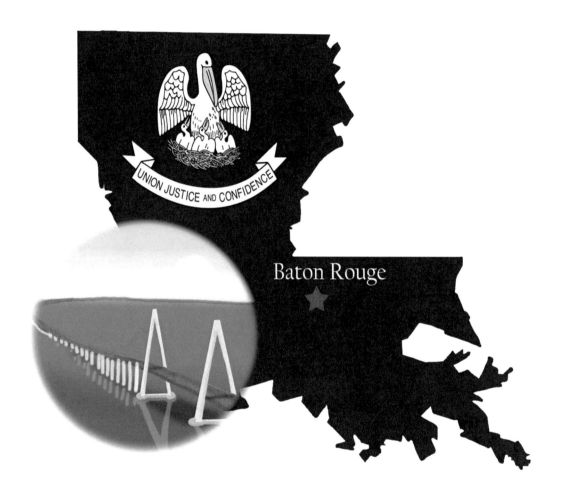

Baton Rouge

Music, culture and spicy food
are all a part of the Louisiana mood.
Hot and humid, the animals don't mind.
Pelicans, alligators and crawfish you will find!

(Model: Evelyn, DeRidder)

MAINE

Augusta

Maine's wild forests are rich with
moose and pine trees.
As you travel down the mountains,
boats and lobsters fill the seas!

(Model: Luke, Warren)

MARYLAND

Annapolis

Right on the coast and down by the bay,
fisherman haul in blue crab each day.
Toward the mountains and Mason-Dixon Line,
the scenery you'll see here is simply divine!

(Model: Nora, Havre de Grace)

MASSACHUSETTS

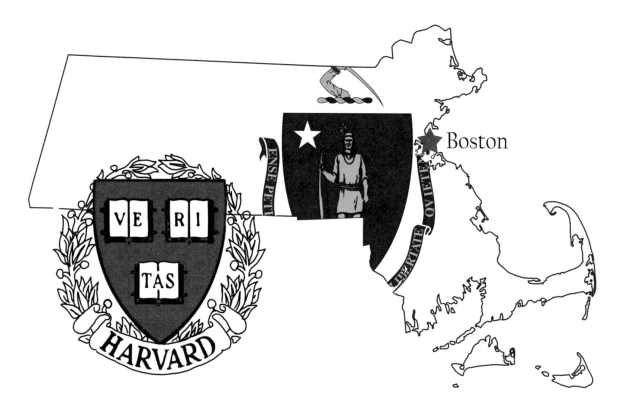

Boston

Where the Mayflower landed and
pilgrims first explored,
in this "State of Firsts" you will never get bored.
Whether visiting Fenway Park
or one of its numerous bays,
to visit all of this state's history
would take many days!

(Model: Chelsea, Chicopee)

MICHIGAN

Lansing

Michigan borders four great lakes,
and has plenty of forests.
With the longest freshwater coastline
in the country,
this state attracts many tourists!

(Model: Parker, Warren)

MINNESOTA

If the ice-cold winters don't scare you away,
the thousands of lakes will sure make you stay.
Minneapolis and Saint Paul
are the heart of this state,
while the largest Mall of America
keeps shoppers' feeling great!

(Model: Maliah, Ortonville)

MISSISSIPPI

Jackson

Named after our country's longest river,
the shores lined with magnolia trees
can really deliver.
Watch out for catfish found in the streams,
a place like this is found
only in fishermen's dreams!

(Model: Chandler, McComb)

MISSOURI

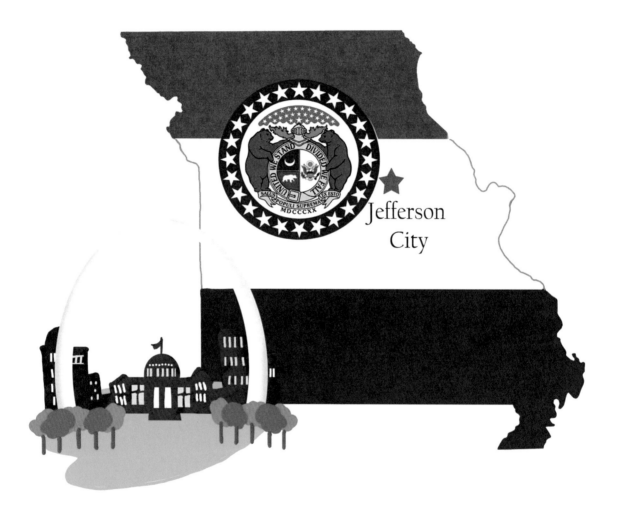

Jefferson City

The Gateway Arch and Twain's National Forest
are features of this state.
And if you're looking for good music and food,
Branson and Kansas City are great!

(Model: Harper, St. Louis)

MONTANA

Helena

Grizzly bears and bighorn sheep
grace this mountainous state.
Rich in copper, gold and silver,
dig through the slate and the treasure is great!

(Model : Kellan, Billings)

NEBRASKA

Lincoln

Nebraska is called the Cornhusker State,
with fields of corn galore.
With big beautiful trees and tons of state pride,
there's a lot here to adore!

(Models: Hope and Hannah, O'Neill)

NEVADA

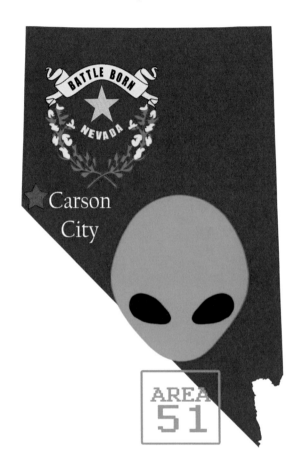

Once famous for its silver
now produces the most gold,
visiting this state may never get old.
With all of the entertainment, dining, and shops,
Las Vegas never sleeps
and the nightlife never stops!

(Model: Gabe, Las Vegas)

NEW HAMPSHIRE

Concord

This state has tons of granite quarries,
but is better known for mining gravel and sand.
Whether visiting Mount Washington
or White Mountain National Forest,
cider donuts must be in the plan!

(Model: William, Nashua)

NEW JERSEY

Trenton

New Jersey is where the gardens grow.
Corn and tomatoes, row by row!
If you like the sea, head to the shore.
Fish, diners, and people galore!

(Model: Addison, Swedesboro)

NEW MEXICO

Santa Fe

INTERNATIONAL
UFO MUSEUM
RESEARCH CENTRE

Full of fascinating places and multicultural faces;
Santa Fe is the oldest capital in the nation.
The Pow Wows here can't be beat,
they happen all year round,
even in the summer heat!

(Model: Parker, Albuquerque)

NEW YORK

The empire state is one of a kind,
large cities and skyscrapers is what you will find.
But past the crowds and city fountains,
you reach the Adirondack Mountains!

(Model: Francesca, New York City)

NORTH CAROLINA

Raleigh

Visiting the Biltmore mansion or the beaches
in the Outer Banks,
climbing Grandfather Mountain the nature here
definitely outranks.
This state also harvests peanuts and
sweet potatoes galore
and that's not all, there's plenty more!

(Model: Lian, Raleigh)

NORTH DAKOTA

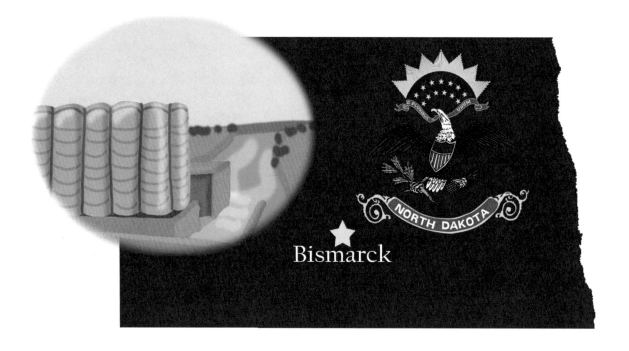

Bismarck

The Peace Garden State with its Great Plains,
is every bison and bobcats wish.
And Red River Valley and Devils Lake are
home to more than seventy species of fish!

(Model: Rhett, Washburn)

OHIO

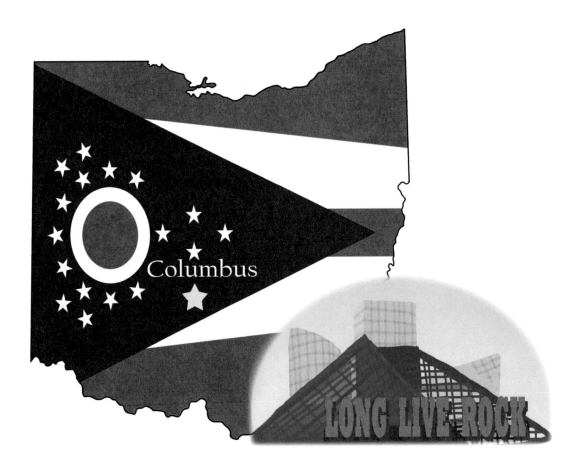

Columbus

LONG LIVE ROCK

The Buckeye State is known for more than just trees,
like the five-mile Serpent Mound that
visitors come to see.
Home to the first man on the moon and the
Rock and Roll Hall of Fame
if you visit this state you'll be glad you came!

(Model: Reece, Kenton)

OKLAHOMA

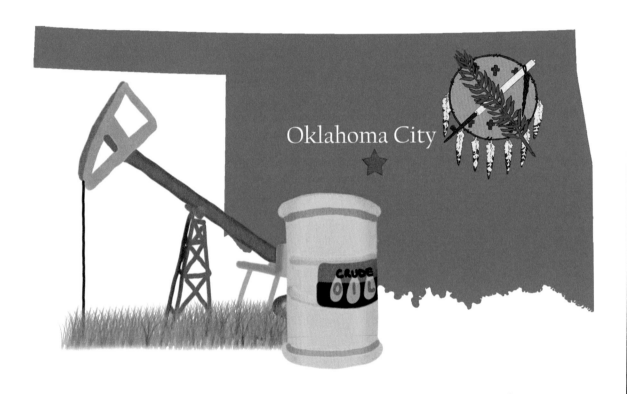

Oklahoma City

Right in the middle of Tornado Alley,
these big twisters don't dilly dally.
The Wichita Mountains lie to the southeast
and this state is home to 39 tribes, at least!

(Model: Luca,Tulsa)

OREGON

Home to Hells Canyon and Crater Lake,
both are the country's deepest.
The Columbia Plateau makes up
half of this state,
and a street in Oregon City
is the world's steepest!

(Model: Jackson, Hillsboro)

PENNSYLVANIA

Harrisburg

National forests, mountains, and farmland,
this is where our independence was planned.
The biggest city, Philadelphia, is known very well,
for its cheesesteaks, pretzels, and the Liberty Bell!

(Model: Kendall, York)

RHODE ISLAND

Providence

Our country's smallest state,
but the ocean views are certainly first rate!
Narragansett Bay is famous for its clams;
some can be huge weighing hundreds of grams!

(Model: Lizzie, Jamestown)

SOUTH CAROLINA

Columbia

A southeastern state that touches the ocean;
its miles of shoreline are always in motion.
Wild pigs and river otters are often seen here
and if you visit,
don't forget your fishing gear!

(Model: Jude, Charleston)

SOUTH DAKOTA

Rolling prairies and American bison
stretch from Sioux Falls to rapid city.
The scenery in Badlands National Park and
Mount Rushmore sure make this state pretty!

(Model: Renner, Sioux Falls)

TENNESSEE

Nashville

Nashville is known as the heart of country music,
with wonderful tunes from the acoustic.
Fort Knox and the mountains are a sight to see,
but the Grand Ole Opry is where you should be!

(Model: Lila, Nashville)

TEXAS

Austin

In a state this big,
the Alamo, Space Center, or Big Bend National Park
could all be your favorite attraction.
The Lone Star state, home to the Texas Longhorn
and the armadillo,
sure has lots of action!

(Model: Landrie, Azle)

UTAH

Elk roam the tall mountains in this state,
but travel south and it will be a much warmer date.
The red sandstone arches are a beautiful creation,
some of the nicest in the nation!

(Model: Gabriella, Spanish Fork)

VERMONT

Montpelier

With syrup harvested from their maple trees,
this sweet place is sure to please.
Vermont's skiing is some of the best,
with miles of mountains there's no time to rest!

(Model: Makenna, Londonderry)

VIRGINIA

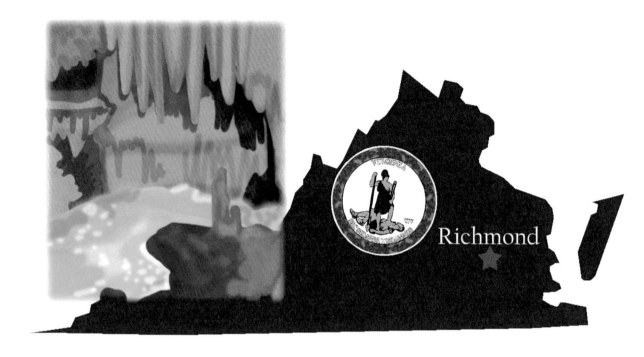

Richmond

Virginia changes as you go.
Mountains, caves, and rivers flow.
As history does know,
this state is where the first colonists would go!

(Model: Grayson, Roanoke)

WASHINGTON D.C.

Our Nation's Capital and home to the President,
this district of our country is actually not a state.
A bounty of embassies, museums, and monuments,
visiting here you'd have a lot on your plate!

(Model: Lizzie, Washington D.C.)

WASHINGTON

Olympia

Rain forests, farmland, deserts, and beaches;
the Evergreen State has so much to see.
If you travel to Yakima Nation,
you'll see thousands of wild horses roam free!

(Model: Brooklyn, Battle Ground)

WEST VIRGINIA

Charleston

Berkeley Castle, Seneca Caverns and
Big Bend Tunnel are in the mountain state.
Its Civil War history, coal production,
and Golden Delicious apples are all top rate!

(Model: Kannon, Wheeling)

WISCONSIN

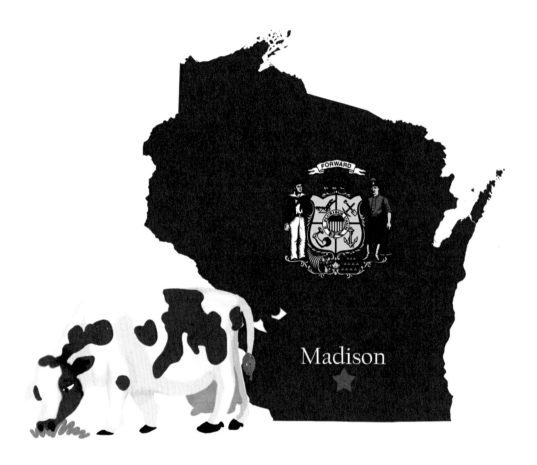

Madison

With Lake Michigan to the east,
this land is mainly known for dairy and the climate
here is continental so the winters can be scary.
Known as "America's Dairyland,"
the lakes, parks and beautiful bays here
definitely weren't planned!

(Model: Adeline, Kaukauna)

WYOMING

Cheyenne

Yellowstone National Park opened in 1872,
and the Wild West rodeo is what
people come to do.
See the geysers erupt if you visit at night time,
and if you're feeling brave,
venture into a coal mine!

(Model: Paxton, Casper)

Photographers and Landmarks

Photographers

Alaska – Relic Photographic

Colorado – Carmen Morales, JCM Photography

Delaware – Taren Cooper Photography

Georgia – My Only Focus Photography

Michigan – Sara Demick Photography

Mississippi – Amanda Elchos Smith

New Hampshire – Sandra Burke

New Mexico – Cam Storie Photography

North Carolina – Katelyn McKay Photography

North Dakota – Brandy Lee Photography

Ohio – Jennie Good Photographs

Vermont – Hubert Schriebl

Washington, D.C. – Keyla S. Photography

Wyoming – Kristian Rhae Proudfoot

Landmarks

Connecticut – Mystic Drawbridge

Maryland – Concord Point Lighthouse

Missouri – Gateway Arch

New Hampshire – Contoocook Railroad Covered Bridge

New Mexico – Sandia Mountains

New York – Rockefeller Center, New York City

Oregon – Multnomah Falls

Rhode Island – Castle Hill Lighthouse, Beavertail Lighthouse

South Carolina –Mount Pleasant Memorial Waterfront Park

Vermont – Stratton Mountain Resort

Washington D.C. – Lincoln Memorial and Reflecting Pool on the National Mall

Devon, a former teacher, and Lindsay, an avid reader, both discovered that while there are thousands of educational books about the United States, there aren't that many that include children with disabilities. As passionate advocates within the disability and Down syndrome communities, both Devon and Lindsay envision a world that includes more children and adults like their daughters, Addison and Charlotte, in literature. Their goal is to help pave the way for other authors and for their children to be able to see themselves, or characters like them, in more books and educational materials. They want their children to grow up in a world where they can envision themselves in these stories and see others who look like them within the literary world. With imagination and reading being so critical for the development of children of all abilities, this book is a beacon of hope that more reading materials will include those within the disability community and show all children that they can do anything they set their mind to.

Made in the USA
Middletown, DE
22 April 2019